Book 8
Motion Moves Machines

A wonderful example of a machine in motion!

Contents

Introduction	Motion Moves Machines	3
Chapter 1	Why Things Move	4
Chapter 2	Easy Does It!	10
Chapter 3	Compound Machines	18
Chapter 4	Technology Today — Around the World Non-stop	21
Check Up	Alberta Einstein's Brain Tester	22
Don't Gloss Over the Glossary!		24
Indexed!		25

Eric Einstein uses a machine to set Alberta in motion. (Experiment No 1 - Eric's first)

Introduction

Motion Moves Machines

How did they do it in the old days?

Do You Know...
- why things move?
- what work is?
- how machines make work easier?
- about simple and compound machines?

Chapter 1   Why Things Move

■ How do force, friction, and inertia affect motion?

Nothing moves or changes direction by itself. Something has to make it start moving or keep it moving. If it stops or changes direction, something causes this to happen.

Forces Cause Motion Motion is caused by a force. Any change in speed or direction of motion is also caused by a force. A **force** is a push or pull.

The effect of a force on an object depends on two things. One is the size of the force, and the other is the direction of the force. Look at the picture below. What would happen to the pulling force if more dogs were added? What would happen if the person in the back pulled the sled in the opposite direction of the dogs?

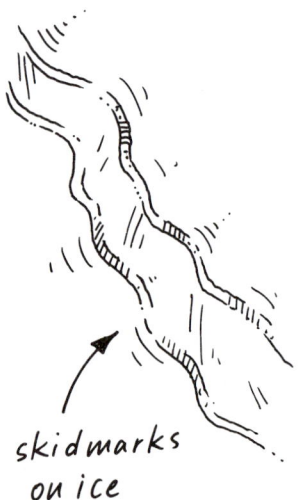
skidmarks on ice

Another Push-Me-Pull-You in Action.

The dogs provide the force that causes the sled to move.

What force pulls the skydivers down?

A dog sled moves because of the pulling force of the dogs. If the dogs have a hard time, a person can help by pushing on the sled.

One of the most important forces for causing motion is gravity. **Gravity** is the force that pulls all things toward the centre of the earth. The skydivers are being pulled to the earth by gravity. Throw a ball up and it, too, will be pulled back to the earth by gravity.

You may be surprised to know that a pulling force exists between any two objects. Even small objects are pulling on each other. However, objects with the most mass have the greatest pulling force. For example, the earth has incredible mass. For this reason, its pulling force is so strong that the pull of other objects does not seem to exist.

Forces Resist Motion Not all pushes and pulls cause motion. In fact, one force actually resists motion. The force is friction. **Friction** is a force that resists motion between two things that rub against each other. Friction is present wherever two surfaces touch.

The effects of friction are all around you. Friction between your feet and the ground keeps your feet from sliding out from under you when you walk. Friction is the force that makes most moving objects stop. Friction is used by brakes to stop bicycles, cars, trains, and planes. The drawing below shows how the disc brakes on a car use friction.

1. In a moving car, the pads do not touch the rotating disc attached to the wheel. The disc and wheel turn freely.

2. When the driver pushes the brake pedal, force moves to brake pads through fluid in a tube. The force pushes the pads against the rotating disc. The pads squeeze the disc from each side.

3. Friction from the pads causes the disc and the wheel to stop rotating. This slows the car down.

How disc brakes work

What does the parachute do to the moving car's inertia?

Objects Resist Change in Motion

You have learned that a force is needed to make an object move. You have also learned that a force is needed to slow down or stop a moving object. These forces are needed because of a certain property that all matter has. The property is called inertia (in-ersha). **Inertia** causes all matter that is moving to stay in motion. It also causes all matter that is not moving to stay at rest.

If you have ridden in a car, you have probably experienced inertia. When a car quickly starts to move, you may have had the feeling of being pushed back in the seat. Your body had the tendency to stay at rest while the car started to move forward. The motion of the car caused the car seat to push forward against your motionless body.

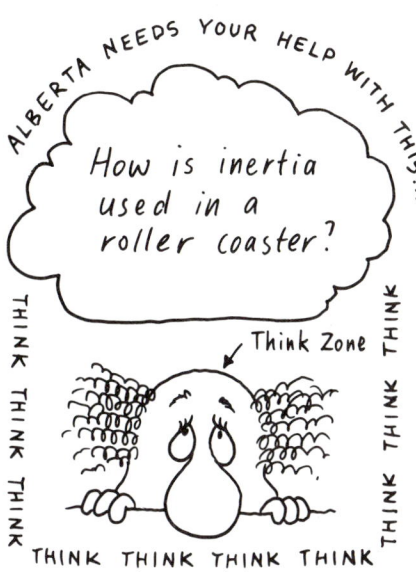

Belt up for safety's sake.

Once the car is moving, your body moves with it. If the car comes to a sudden stop, your body tends to stay in motion. Inertia keeps your body moving forward. Inertia is the reason you should wear a seat belt.

The amount of inertia an object has depends on the object's mass. The more mass an object has, the more inertia it has. The ships in the picture have much inertia. Because they have so much inertia, it takes a lot of force to make them move or to stop them once they are moving.

Which ship has the most inertia?

Have you ever tried to push a heavy object? The heavier the object, the more inertia you have to overcome before the object begins to move. Inertia also makes it harder to stop heavier objects once they are moving.

Eric Einstein's Guide to Games for those Suffering from Inertia
(of the motionless kind)

1 Count the skin cells on your big toe.

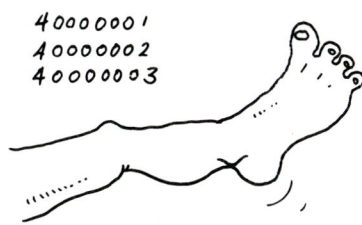

2 Watch your hair grow.

3 See how much time passes between blinks.

4 Set a world record for couch potatoes.

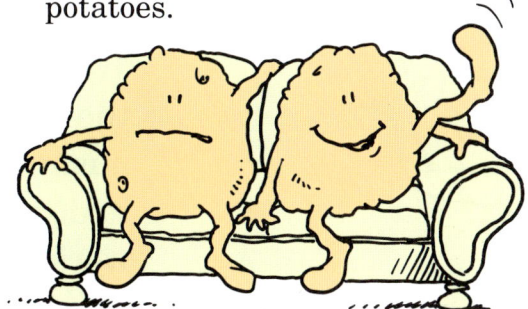

5 Set another world record for the slowest possible movement — try beckoning with your index finger.

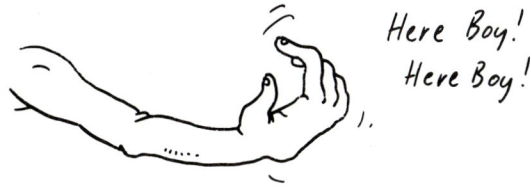

6 Teach your eyes how to smile.

7 Record the rumblings of your stomach on tape.

8 Make your own confetti — draw 9 million little circles on paper and cut them out.

Chapter 2 Easy Does It!

■ How are force and motion related to work and machines?

What does the word "work" make you think of? Chances are different people in your class will have different answers. Do any answers involve some kind of push or pull?

What do you use to do work? Again, different people will have different answers. Many might say they use tools or machines. In this chapter, you will find out about work and how machines can make work easier to do.

fingers itching to work

If something does not move, no work is done.

Fingers in Motion

Work and Motion When scientists use the word "work", it means more than just pushing or pulling. To a scientist, the only way to do work is to make something move. All work involves motion. If something does not move, no work is done. **Work** is applying a force to move an object through a distance. Think of all the things that you make move.

What kind of work is each worker doing?

You pull a switch or push a button to turn on a light. You open a door or window. You move your arm to throw a ball. In each case, you were doing work. Maybe it was not very hard work, but — each time — you used a force to make something move.

Which boat takes more work to move?

When something moves, the amount of work done depends on two things. One is the amount of force, and the other is the distance the object moves. Look at the pictures of the boats. The boat on the right is heavier. It takes more force, and therefore more work, to move the boat on the right. It would also take a lot more work to move either boat 100 metres than it would to move it 50 metres.

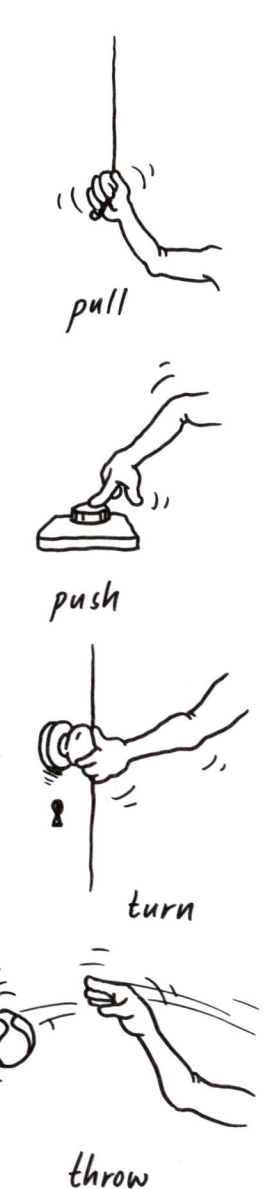

The ghostly arm strikes again.

Simple Machines Doing work takes force. Sometimes, work takes more force than you have. For this reason, machines are used to make work easier.

When you think of machines, you probably think of things such as tractors and motors. However, they have many parts. Many of the machines that you use each day do not have many moving parts. These machines are called **simple machines.** The pictures show examples of the six kinds of simple machines.

Pulley

Lever

Inclined plane

Wedge

Wheel and axle

Screw

Using a lever

All simple machines require a force to do work. The force that is used to do work is called the **effort**. The effort is used to move an object. The object moved by the effort is called a **resistance**.

Look at the picture above. The worker is using a crowbar to pry a board loose from a deck. The crowbar is being used as a lever. The board is the resistance. The effort is the amount of force the worker must use to make the board move. The crowbar makes it easier for the worker to pry the board loose.

Machines can be used to make work easier. They are often used to reduce the amount of effort needed to do work. They can also be used to change the direction of a force. With some machines, for example, a downward effort allows you to move a resistance up.

Using a pulley clothesline

Changing the Direction of Force

The pulley and the lever are two simple machines that can change the direction of force. Look at the picture of the man hanging clothes on the pulley clothesline. By pulling the rope on top, he causes the rope on the bottom to move away from him. The clothes then move toward the pulley at the other end of the clothesline. The clothesline pulley changes the direction of the force that the man is using to do work.

Now look at the clowns in the drawing below. A lever is part of their circus act. One clown jumps down onto one end of the lever. The clown on the other end of the lever is hurled up into the air by the downward force of the first clown. The lever has changed a downward force to an upward force.

Getting some leverage?

Using Machines to Reduce Effort

A simple machine can help move a heavy object with less effort. Think, for example, what happens when a person gets a flat tyre on a car. The car is too heavy to lift. But by using a jack, the person can lift the car and change the tyre.

How does the longer handle help do work?

The handle of a jack is a lever. The handle changes the amount of effort needed to do the same amount of work and raise the car. A jack with a longer handle takes less effort than a jack with a shorter handle.

Look at the drawings of the car above. The end of the longer handle travels farther than the end of the shorter handle. The effort decreases with the longer handle, but the distance increases. Therefore the amount of work stays the same.

What's this?

Yes, it's a car tyre going flat!

A wheel and axle in disguise as a kitchen tap.

The lever is not the only simple machine that can reduce effort by increasing distance. If you have ever tried to turn a tap without a handle, you know how hard it is to do. The handle of the tap connects to a stem that reaches down into the water pipe. The handle plus the stem form a simple machine called a wheel and axle.

When the handle of a tap is turned, the stem also turns. However, the handle and the stem move different distances. Let's say you measure the distance around the handle and around the stem. You may find that for every complete turn, the handle travels ten centimetres farther than the stem. The greater distance travelled by the handle reduces the effort needed to move the stem.

How a wheel and axle reduces effort.

Brain-teaser Time!

How does friction affect the amount of work that is done by a machine?

Answer: Friction reduces how well a machine works by increasing the effort needed to get work done.

Chapter 3   Compound Machines

■ How are compound machines similar to and different from simple machines?

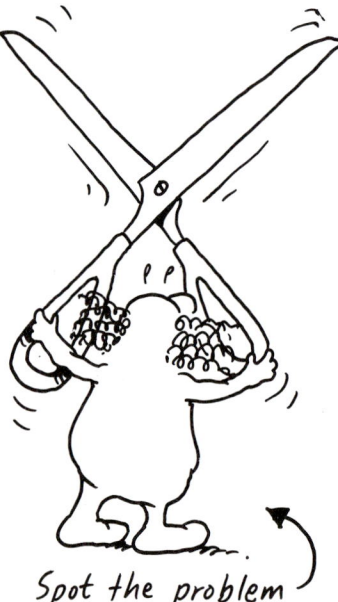

Spot the problem

Eric and Alberta like to make up hard questions. They try to trap each other. Eric held up a pair of scissors. "How many machines are in these scissors?" he asked.

Alberta took the scissors and worked with them. Finally she said, "The two moving parts of the scissors are levers. The edge of each part is another machine called a wedge."

Eric smiled. Alberta was right — as usual!

Two Machines in One Machines that are made of more than one simple machine are called **compound machines.** Scissors are a compound machine because they are made of levers and wedges.

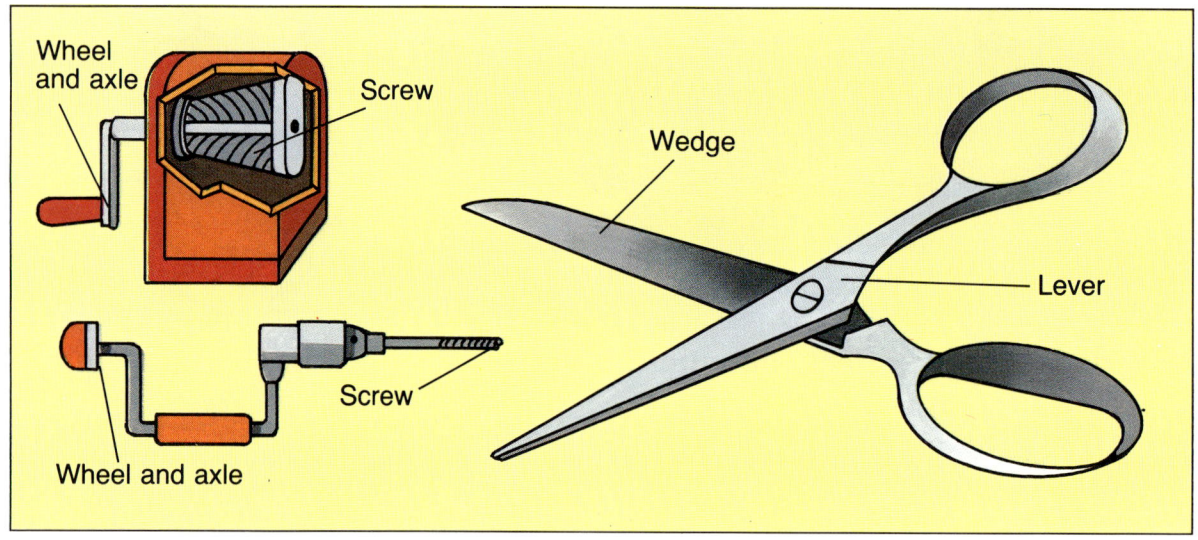

Some Compound Machines

There are different kinds of scissors. Some cut paper. Some cut wire. Shears, which are like scissors, cut branches of trees. Look at the pictures of the different kinds of scissors and shears. Compare their shapes and sizes.

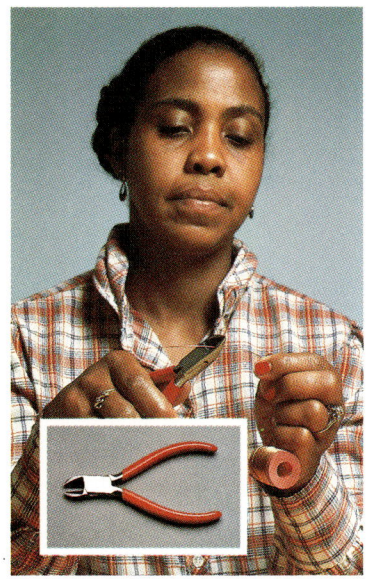 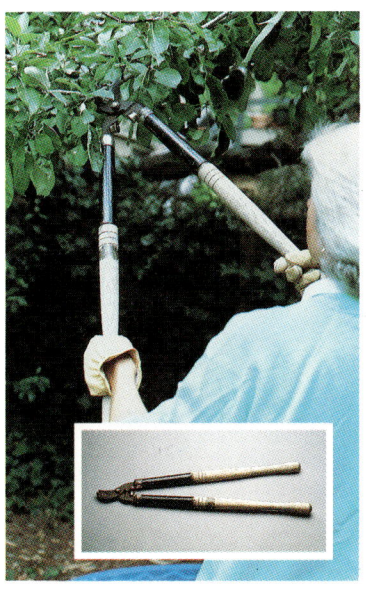 

Different kinds of scissors are used for different work.

It is hard to cut through a thick branch. Look at the shears in the picture in the middle. They have long handles. This reduces the effort needed to cut through a hard branch.

Compare the other scissors in the pictures. The handles of the wire cutter are longer than the blades. This reduces the effort needed to cut tough metal. Scissors that cut cloth have shorter handles and longer blades. Cloth is easy to cut. Also, the longer blades make longer cuts with each cutting motion.

There are no short cuts for sharp cuts!

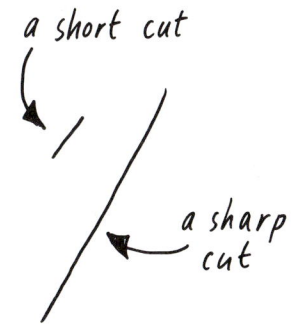

Tailor-made magic.

19

Many Machines in One Some machines are made of many machines that work together. A bicycle is made of many machines. The wheels, brakes, gears, and handlebars are types of simple machines. Look at the drawing below. It explains how different parts of a bicycle work as simple machines.

The handlebars are part of a wheel and axle used to steer the bicycle.

The hand brakes are levers that apply a force to stop the bicycle.

The pedals are a wheel and axle that receive the force from the rider's feet and legs.

The chain transfers the force from the pedals to the gears.

The gears transfer the force from the chain to the rear wheel. They change the number of times the rear wheel turns as the rider pedals the bicycle.

Machines in a bicycle

Chapter 4   Technology Today

Voyager

Around the World — Non-stop!

Look at the picture of the aeroplane Voyager. Most likely, you have never seen an aeroplane that looks anything like Voyager. It has a very special design. Everything about Voyager was done with one thing in mind: to be the first plane to fly around the world without stopping, on a single supply of fuel.

The wings of Voyager are as long as those of a jetliner. They help the plane use the wind as much as possible. This saves fuel. The plane is built out of material that is very light. This also saves fuel.

To make it around the world, the two pilots had to make their fuel last as long as possible. They needed to make their machine work the best it could. They needed to reduce friction. They needed to reduce the amount of effort that would come from the engines, which run on fuel.

Think About It

Voyager took off on December 14, 1986. It completed its trip around the world (41,600 kilometres) without refuelling, in 9 days, 3 minutes, and 44 seconds. Was Voyager's record good only for the people who flew the plane? Why or why not?

Check Up

Alberta Einstein's Brain Tester

"Eric, you need a brain check-up! Heh! Heh!"

> **Summary**
> - Force affects the motion of an object.
> - The motion of an object tends to stay the same because of inertia.
> - Work involves using force to move an object.
> - Machines can change the direction of a force.
> - Machines can make work easier by reducing the effort that is needed to do work.
> - Machines are classified as simple and compound.

Science Ideas

1. Make a list from **a** to **d**. Tell whether each statement is fact or opinion.
   a. Gravity is a force that pulls all things toward the centre of the earth.
   b. Ice skating is much more fun than roller skating.
   c. Levers and pulleys are examples of simple machines.
   d. Levers are better than pulleys.

2. Make a list from **a** to **f**. Write the name of each simple machine

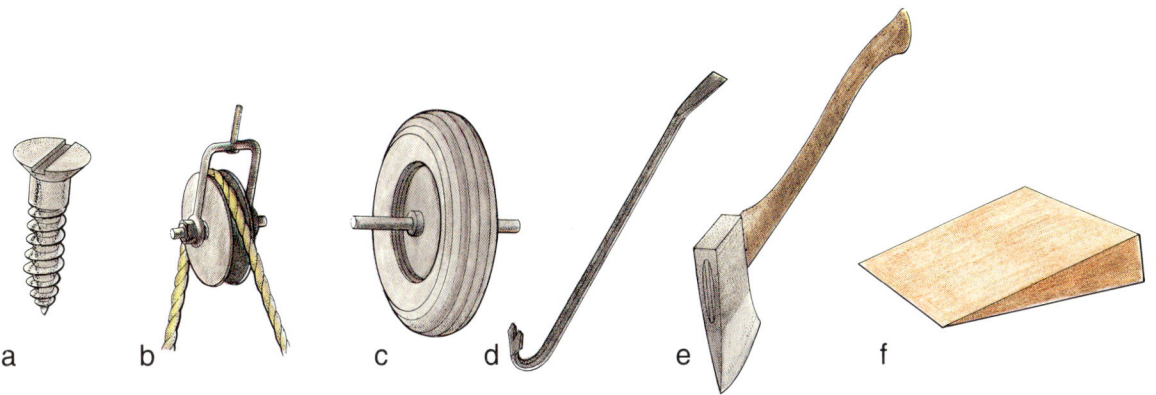

a b c d e f

3 Data bank

Use the table on the right to answer the following questions.

1. Which was invented first — the vacuum cleaner, lawnmower, or electric washing machine?

2. What was the year in which the helicopter was invented?

4 Problem Solving

Some nice neighbours give you four chairs and a table for your new treehouse. You need both hands when going up the narrow ladder to the entrance. Knowing this, how do you plan to get the furniture into the treehouse? Draw a diagram of your plan.

Machine inventions	
Machine	Year first built
Aeroplane	1903
Automobile	1885
Bicycle	1816
Helicopter	1939
Jet-propelled aircraft	1930
Lawnmower	1831
Motorcycle	1884
Submarine	1891
Trolley car (electric)	1884
Vacuum cleaner	1907
Washing machine (electric)	1901

Don't Gloss over the Glossary!

compound machine — a machine that is made up of more than one machine

effort — a force that is used to do work

exists — to be or to live

force — a push or pull that causes motion or changes its speed or direction

friction — a force that resists motion between two things that rub together

gravity — a force that pulls objects towards each other

inertia — something that causes all matter that is moving to stay in motion, or all matter that is not moving to stay at rest

motion — movement

motionless — without moving

resistance — the object moved by an effort

simple machine — an object with few moving parts that is used to do work

work — the act of using force to move an object through a distance

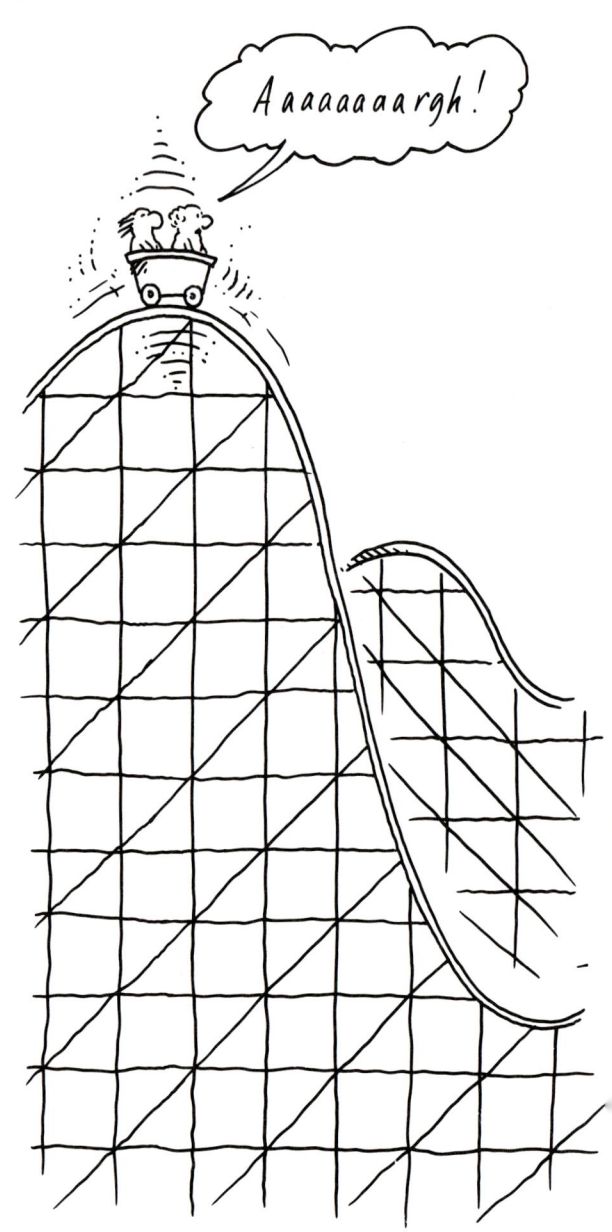

A moment of inertia